# The Ultimate Guide to Dance Team Tryout Secrets
## Jr./Sr. High
## 3rd Edition

Summer Adoue-Johansen

**Netherfield House Press**

Copyright © 2003-2012 by Summer Adoue-Johansen

All rights reserved. No part of this publication may be reproduced, distributed, or transmitted in any form or by any means, or stored in a database or retrieval system, without the prior written permission from the publisher, except as permitted under the U.S. Copyright Act of 1976.

Netherfield House Press

www.NetherfieldHousePress.com

Printed in the United States of America

ISBN 978-1-935649-04-5

Library of Congress Control Number: 2010926303

**Library of Congress subject headings:**

Dance -- Auditions -- United States

Dance -- Juvenile literature

Dance teams -- Juvenile literature

Dance

Editing, cover and layout design: Melissa Darnell

Creative Commons 2.0 Photo Credits:

Pg. 2 and 77 photos courtesy of JMRosenfeld@Flickr

Pg. 15 photo courtesy of lu_lu@Flickr

Pg. 71 and 82 photos courtesy of Tulane Public Relations@Flickr

Pg. 79 photo courtesy of tibchris@Flickr

Pg. 96 photo courtesy of wei li graphic designer@Flickr

Pg. 104 photo courtesy of RogueSun Media@Flickr

Pg. 112 photo courtesy of quinn.anya@Flickr

Pg. 124 photo courtesy of allspice1@Flickr

Pg. 133 photo courtesy of Will Folsom@Flickr

All other photos courtesy of SavannahAnn McMillan

# Table of Contents

## ⭐ Chapter 1: Research the Team and Its Tryout Process ...... 1
- About The Team ...... 2
  - Where does the dance team perform? ...... 3
  - Are there tryouts for each routine performed? ...... 3
  - Does the team produce a spring show? ...... 4
  - Does the team compete during contest season? ...... 4
  - What kind of style does the team perform? ...... 5
  - How much does it cost to be a member? ...... 5
  - Is there a team trip each year? ...... 6
  - What is the team's typical practice schedule? ...... 6
- About the Tryouts ...... 7
- Tryout Requirements ...... 9
- The Team's Style ...... 12
- Mentoring ...... 13

## ⭐ Chapter 2: Preparing Yourself Physically ...... 14
- Getting Into Shape ...... 15
  - Sample Cardio Program ...... 18
  - Abdominal Stretch ...... 21
  - Regular Abdominal Crunches ...... 22
  - Lying Side Bends ...... 24
  - The Lift ...... 26
  - The Squeeze ...... 28
  - Planks ...... 30
- Becoming Flexible ...... 32
  - Toe Touch Drill #1 ...... 52
  - Toe Touch Drill #2 ...... 54
  - Toe Touch Drill #3 ...... 55
  - Sitting High Kick Drill ...... 57
  - Front Splits ...... 65

- Center Splits ................................................................. 67
- Kicks ............................................................................ 68
- Step Kicks .................................................................... 72

Developing Dance Technique ............................................ 74
Probable Moves ................................................................. 76
- Turns ........................................................................... 77
- Leaps ........................................................................... 79

Practice Makes Perfect ...................................................... 80

## ⭐ Chapter 3: Preparing Yourself Mentally ........................... 81

Confidence ......................................................................... 82
- Confidence Vs. Ego ..................................................... 84

Focus .................................................................................. 84
Motivation .......................................................................... 85

## ⭐ Chapter 4: Preparing Your Appearance ............................ 89

Audition Day Outfit .......................................................... 90
- Leotards ....................................................................... 90
- Fit ................................................................................ 92
- T-shirts and Shorts ..................................................... 93
- Jazz Pants .................................................................... 93
- Underneath It All ....................................................... 94
- Shoes ........................................................................... 95

Makeup .............................................................................. 96
- Foundation and Blush ................................................ 97
- Eyes ............................................................................. 97
- Lips .............................................................................. 99

Hair ................................................................................... 100
Warm-ups ........................................................................ 100

## Chapter 5: Prepare the Paperwork .................................................. 102
Dates and Deadlines ............................................................................. 103
Time Management ................................................................................ 104
Working with Teachers ......................................................................... 105

## Chapter 6: Tryout Practice Day Tips ............................................. 107
Length of Time ...................................................................................... 108
Preparation ............................................................................................ 108
Getting Down to Business .................................................................... 109
Attitude .................................................................................................. 110
Positions Please .................................................................................... 111
Focus ..................................................................................................... 112
Memorization Tips ................................................................................ 113
Turn It ON! ............................................................................................ 114
It's All in the Details ............................................................................. 115
What to Wear ........................................................................................ 116
Breathe! ................................................................................................. 118

## Chapter 7: Audition Day Tips ........................................................ 119
The Night Before Tryouts ..................................................................... 120
- Triple Check It .................................................................................. 121
- Beauty Items ..................................................................................... 122
- Dancer Fuel ....................................................................................... 123

Tryouts Day .......................................................................................... 124
Sample Judges' Score Sheet ................................................................. 128
Callbacks ............................................................................................... 130

## Chapter 8: After the New Team Announcements ......................... 132

## About the Author ............................................................................. 137

# CHAPTER 1

## Research the Team and Its Tryout Process

**S**o, you are interested in trying out for a dance team? The first thing I have to say to you is: CONGRATULATIONS!! Dance teams, at any age or level, are a fantastic way to help you gain many advantages in life that will carry you towards a successful future. Some of those advantages include self-respect, respect for others, and the ability to work as a team. I can absolutely and positively say that being part of several dance teams was the best thing that I could have ever done

# Ch. 1

### The Ultimate Guide to Dance Team Tryout Secrets

for myself. I commend you on taking the first step in seeking information on dance team tryouts.

## ☆About The Team ☆

The first activity you need to do when interested in joining a dance team is to do some investigation. You might be surprised when you find out how much is really involved in being a member of a team! All teams are certainly not the same, and they all have different aspects that make each team unique and special.

When it comes time to think about auditions, junior and high school dance teams typically will begin to recruit for new members. Sometimes

## Research the Team and Its Tryout Process

CH. 1

an officer or veteran member will occupy a booth at school to answer questions, or you can always go straight to the team director for information. The important questions listed below will give you a strong knowledge base to guide you in your decision about joining the team.

## Where does the dance team perform?

This is important to know because some teams perform only at football and basketball games. There may also be several community events at which the team will perform, such as town parades or Christmas celebrations. This will give you some idea of the time commitment that the team requires.

## Are there tryouts for each routine performed?

Seldom does the audition process end with the actual team tryouts. It is very typical to learn a routine on Monday for a Friday football game and audition for the performance on Wednesday. Some teams also have policies that only new team members have to audition. This policy varies from team to team, so learn all you can about the audition requirements throughout the year.

# CH. 1 — The Ultimate Guide to Dance Team Tryout Secrets

## Does the team produce a spring show?

A spring show production has become extremely popular with junior and high school dance teams and can involve everything from team, solo, and ensemble performances to productions that involve other school organizations or community groups. Needless to say, this is quite an undertaking and will require a great deal of time and team effort to make the production a success. Make sure you are ready and willing to give the kind of commitment that is required for such a production.

## Does the team compete during contest season?

Dance competitions are a very popular activity for teams to engage in during the winter or spring months. Most teams will perform three team routines, with the officers performing an additional two to three routines. In addition, there are opportunities to perform ensembles, duets, and solos. Competitions in recent years have exploded in popularity and attendance. As a competition judge for many years and more recently as a contest administrator, I have been amazed at the ever-growing size of contests and the creativity of the

## Research the Team and Its Tryout Process

teams. This is a very exciting time for dance groups, but you need to realize that there is a great deal of hard work and many hours that are required in producing a winning routine.

## What kind of style does the team perform?

Is it precision dance or more stylized? Do they prefer high kick routines rather than modern dance, or does the team have a pom squad style? This question is VERY important because you need to do an evaluation of what type of style you are most comfortable dancing and whether or not the team is a "good fit" for you.

## How much does it cost to be a member?

There is almost always a monetary cost involved in being a dance team member. The fees will typically include practice wear, camp tuition (possibly two camps for officers), contest fees, costume fees, etc. This should not scare you off, however. Many teams will fundraise, sometimes several times throughout the year, to raise money. Fundraisers have become more creative and successful over the past few years, and some teams can even raise enough money to finance their entire team for certain items such as costumes for contest or spring show. Additionally,

**CH. 1** — The Ultimate Guide to Dance Team Tryout Secrets

school districts vary in what they will or will not pay for when it comes to dance team activities. Fortunately, many districts are realizing the growing popularity of contests and spring shows and will have money earmarked for those events. Therefore, even though there is a cost involved, many teams try to minimize the costs as much as possible.

### Is there a team trip each year?

Some teams take an annual team trip, which may add to the cost of being on that team. Some teams consider traveling to competitions as their annual team trip. Still other teams alternate their trip years with competition years. If there is a team trip, there is always a great deal of fundraising that is involved to minimize the costs to the team members.

### What is the team's typical practice schedule?

Does the team practice before school, after, or both? Do they practice on weekends usually? How many days a week, and for how long, do they practice? How does their practice schedule change for each season? Most teams require that you make every practice and have consequences for missing too many of them, such as not getting to perform at the next game. Knowing the team's average practice schedule ahead of time will help you make sure you will be able to attend all the practices if you make the team. This is especially important if you have a job after school. If you do hold a job after school that will conflict with the team's practices, be sure to discuss with your employer the possibility of changing your work days so that you will not have to work and practice on the same days. Do not assume that you will be able to successfully work after practice ends, as sometimes practices run longer than expected, and you will almost certainly be too tired after practice to be able to do your job well at work.

## ★ About the Tryouts ★

There are many varying ways that a dance team will conduct its tryouts. It is important that you familiarize yourself with everything involved so you will not have an unpleasant surprise halfway through the tryouts. The more you know about the process, the more comfortable and confident you will be when the big day arrives.

First of all, you need to learn about the tryout schedule. Does the process span over one week or two, or is it only a few days? Will the actual tryout day be held over a weekend or after school? Some teams will have a clinic

# CH. 1

## The Ultimate Guide to Dance Team Tryout Secrets

prior to the actual tryout period. If this is the case, it is highly recommended that you attend the clinic. Not only will this give you a chance to evaluate the team, but you can also learn more about the style that they perform and any trademark skills that the team may have.

Ask questions about what types of routines and how many dances will be performed for the judges. It is very common to learn and perform both a jazz routine and a high kick routine. Some teams will also require that you perform both the left and right splits, and possibly execute various leaps or turns. It is a good idea to ask about the skills you will need to perform well in advance of tryouts so that you may prepare accordingly. It is very difficult to learn how to properly execute a switch leap or a double turn without any advance preparation. With the proper time and training, you have a better chance of mastering these difficult skills.

You might also wish to ask how the team will select the new members. Ask the director if he or she can supply you with a blank copy of the score sheet. If you are able to obtain a score sheet, you can get an idea of the breakdown in points and what aspect will be focused on the most, i.e. a higher number of points for the high kick routine versus the jazz

## Research the Team and Its Tryout Process

routine. Also, ask the director if there are a specific number of spots that are available on the team, or if the new members are chosen based on the break in scores.

## ☆Tryout Requirements☆

As mentioned, some teams will hold a dance clinic prior to auditions. However, it is possible that there are additional requirements, such as previous dance training from either a dance studio or a dance class taken in school. Any dance experience you may have always helps, but there are some teams that require a dance class that can be taken as a P.E. elective prior to auditioning for the team. If this is the case, make sure that you find out that information as soon as possible so you can register for the class and fulfill that requirement. Also, ask the director if there is a "reserve" dance team, or pep squad, that is required of new members. Reserve teams and junior varsity teams have grown in popularity over the years with larger high schools. These teams require all new members to have one year in the reserve team to "learn the ropes" before moving on to the varsity team.

# CH. 1 — The Ultimate Guide to Dance Team Tryout Secrets

Dance teams almost always have a grade point average that you must meet to be able to tryout. This requirement is important because you need to have a handle on your grades in order to juggle a hectic practice schedule and complete your schoolwork. Academics should always come first to the dance team, but the dance team should come second ONLY to academics. Make sure you are aware of the team policies and whether or not there is a certain GPA required. This is something you should become aware of early on so you can determine if you can maintain the required grade standard and participate on the team.

Both junior and high school teams will schedule a meeting that you will need to attend with a parent or guardian prior to tryouts. Learn the date and time of this meeting and mark it down on your calendar. At this meeting, the director will go over pertinent information about the team, including the time commitment and cost of team membership. The director will typically also explain the fundraising options and any extra financial help that the school is willing to offer. This meeting is usually mandatory, and it is crucial that both you and your parent or guardian attend. You need to be certain that you and your family can handle all of the aspects that go along with being a member of the team. Additionally,

# Research the Team and Its Tryout Process    CH. 1

it is always helpful to have the support of your family and friends behind you as you go through the tryout process.

Many teams require teachers to complete a recommendation or grade form that you must turn in prior to tryouts. Sometimes the director will supply your teachers with the appropriate form, but this is not always the case. There are teams that require you to ask your teachers for a recommendation and for you to supply the teacher with the required form. Make sure you are well aware of the deadline for the forms to be turned in to the director and do all that is possible to adhere to that schedule. It is always best to get off on the right foot with the director, and missing a deadline right away is certainly not the best way!

Learn about the dress requirements for tryouts as soon as possible. For example, are you required to wear a certain type of leotard and tights, or should you wear a t-shirt and shorts? How about the shoes: jazz shoes or tennis shoes? Does the team require all black for tryouts or a different color? Finally, do the returning members wear something different for tryouts than the new candidates? These are all very important questions that need to be addressed immediately so that you can assemble your tryout uniform well in advance. The last thing you need to worry about on tryout day is if you are wearing the correct attire.

Finally, ask the director for any other information regarding tryouts. As I mentioned earlier, all teams have a different tryout process, and there may be additional requirements that go beyond this information. Knowledge is your best friend in this endeavor, and you will feel empowered when you have all the answers you need.

## ☆ The Team's Style ☆

Some teams have a mixed style and will try a variety of dance types throughout the year. For example, a team may choose high kick and military routines for football season, perform hip hop and pom routines during basketball season, and then perform lyrical and stylized jazz routines during contest season. Of course the opposite might also be true and the team may have a trademark style that they adhere to faithfully.

A good idea to help you assess the team's style is to attend several team performances and see what style they favor. It is also helpful to attend

# Research the Team and Its Tryout Process

## CH. 1

different types of events as described above to see how the style might change from football games to basketball games. If the team does compete, learn what types of routines they are most likely to perform.

You may also want to videotape the team to determine if there is a certain skill or a trademark move that the team executes. By doing this, you can get a great idea of what is to be expected and what you will most likely encounter in the tryout dance. Be mindful of what you need to work on for tryouts and start a practice schedule as soon as possible. It certainly is never too early to start work on that important dance skill that the team requires and then wow the judges at tryouts with your mastery of the element.

## Mentoring

If possible, find a current member of the team who will be willing to help you prepare for tryouts. Most team members would be honored to help you with some of the skills that you need to work on. It is even possible that you could learn a routine that the team has performed in the past. The director of the team might also be able to recommend a team member who is willing to help, so do not be afraid to ask.

# CHAPTER 2

# Preparing Yourself Physically

**W**hen you decide that you are going to audition for a dance team, there are several things you need to do. First of all, prepare yourself physically for the tryouts. If you have not been dancing or exercising on a regular basis, it is important to begin several months in advance to avoid injury and to give yourself the best chance in the tryouts. Dancers need to be strong to execute the difficult movements that are required in a dance routine, and you need to do all that is possible to prepare yourself.

## Preparing Yourself Physically

**CH. 2**

## ⭐ Getting Into Shape ⭐

There are many ways to get into shape, such as power walking, jogging, bicycling, swimming, aerobics classes, etc. Choose what you like to do best so that you can keep up your workout program and enjoy what you are doing. You also do not have to spend a large amount of money on a gym membership to get in shape. There are many ways to create a successful exercise program at home, such as exercise videotapes, a set of stretch bands, or a safe area to run or walk with a good pair of shoes. You might want to consider cross-training, which means doing several different types of exercises on varying days. Not only will this variation keep you interested, but you will also work different parts of your body.

# CH. 2

## The Ultimate Guide to Dance Team Tryout Secrets

Some basic elements for starting a fitness program include having the right clothing and equipment for the type of activity you will be doing. For example, if you wear walking shoes for jogging, you will be susceptible to foot, back, and knee injuries. Also, wear clothing that is appropriate to the exercise you do and the environment you are in. Light, loose-fitting clothing made of natural fibers like cotton help promote air circulation to the skin. This aids in the evaporation of sweat and will help to keep you cooler in hot weather and prevent chilling in cold weather. When you exercise, especially on hot days, you must drink plenty of water to replenish the water you have lost due to perspiration. Six to eight-ounce glasses of water are recommended on normal days, but you should drink more water on hot days or days that you are very active.

It is important to do some type of cardio activity at least three times a week for 30 to 45 minutes within your target heart rate zone. Aerobic activity will help tone your body by increasing muscle size, strength, and flexibility while also burning fat. The key is to find an activity or two that you enjoy and stick with the program. Of course if you are just beginning an exercise program, you must begin at an intensity corresponding to your current level of fitness. Anyone beginning an exercise program for the

## Preparing Yourself Physically

### CH. 2

first time, or after several years of inactivity, should always start slowly and progress gradually. The most important thing you can do is to listen to your body. A good way to measure exertion is by the talk-test. This means that you should be able to comfortably carry on a conversation with a partner without gasping for air. If you cannot do that, decrease your level of activity immediately. Additionally, be aware of certain warning signs such as abnormal heart action, dull pain or heavy pressure in the middle of the chest, or extreme dizziness or disorientation. If any of these occur, stop exercising immediately and contact a physician before resuming your workout program.

By starting slowly and sticking with your program, you will be able to gradually increase the demands on your body. In time you will find that not only will you feel and look better, you will also be able to give 110% in your tryout dance without feeling overly fatigued.

## Sample Cardio Workout

A sample cardiovascular workout could look something like this:

**Warm Up** – At least 5 minutes to increase your heart rate and get the blood flowing to the muscles. After 5 minutes, gradually increase the intensity of your activity. The warm up is one of the most important things you can do to prevent injuries and to exercise more efficiently.

**Aerobic Activity** – If you are just starting a workout program, it is wise to gradually build up to 30 to 45 minutes of exercise. Therefore, you may only be able to do about 10 to 15 minutes of aerobic activity the first week but gradually increase your exercise time every week to increase your endurance and burn more calories.

**Cool Down** – It is important that you do not neglect the cool down, as this time allows your heart rate to gradually slow down and return to normal. To cool down, decrease the level of activity to a slower pace for around 5 minutes. Walking is an ideal cool down and can be used after any exercise routine.

## Preparing Yourself Physically

**CH. 2**

**Stretching** – Stretch the muscles that you have worked for a period of 5 to 10 minutes. Stretch by going to a point of mild tension and then hold the stretch without bouncing for 30-60 seconds. It is imperative that you do not stretch to the point of pain, but you should feel a mild pulling sensation as you stretch the muscle.

You should try to balance a cardiovascular workout with strength training as much as possible. Strength training is important because the stronger you are, the more your balance and coordination will improve. Needless to say, those are two very important elements as a dancer! Strength training will also help your body's metabolism while building stamina, energy, and endurance, and will help to lessen your chances of injury when dancing.

Each body part should be worked at least once a week in strength training. You can accomplish strength training with weight machines, free weights (such as dumbbells), resistance bands (very popular with ballerinas), or your own body weight. Make sure that you do a warm up before you start to increase the blood flow to your muscles. This can be

# CH. 2

## The Ultimate Guide to Dance Team Tryout Secrets

accomplished by a brisk walk or bicycling. The largest muscle groups (your back, chest, and legs) should be worked first. Then proceed to smaller muscle groups (the shoulders, biceps, and triceps). If you are a beginner, you need to start with one set (a fixed number of repetitions) of 8 to 10 repetitions. When you progress, you can increase this to two sets. Lift a weight that is just heavy enough to tire the muscle. Once you can complete 15 to 20 repetitions with ease, slightly increase the weight you are using. Do not hold your breath while you are lifting. Instead, exhale when you pull or lift the weight, and inhale on the release. Finally, it is important that you do not train the same muscle group two days in a row, as your muscles need time to rebuild.

Many of the moves that you will execute as a dancer require an uplifted torso and a strong center. A strong center will allow you to complete difficult turns and leaps, maintain control of your body when you kick, and will also lessen the chance of injury to your lower back. The best way to accomplish this is by developing and strengthening your abdominal muscles. Several basic exercises for toning the abdominal muscles have been included. It is important to remember your form when performing

## Preparing Yourself Physically

**CH. 2**

these exercises so you will get the maximum effect and reduce the chance of injury to the neck and back.

## Abdominal Stretch

Before you begin to exercise your abs, it's important to stretch them first. This helps the muscles loosen up, warm up and get ready to be worked. An easy way to stretch your abs is to lie face down on the floor, then use your hands to push up just your upper body. Be sure to keep your hips on the floor to ensure a good stretch along your abs. Hold for thirty seconds, then you're ready to move on to the abdominal exercises!

## Regular Abdominal Crunches

These are the most common form of abdominal exercise performed to help develop stronger abdominals. While lying on your back, bend your knees.

## Preparing Yourself Physically

With your hands behind your head and keeping your chin off your chest, come up to a 30-degree angle. Make certain that you are not pulling your head; your hands are only there for support because it is your tummy that needs to be doing the work!

## Lying Side Bends

This works the oblique muscles. Begin by lying on your side and resting your head on one hand with your knees bent.

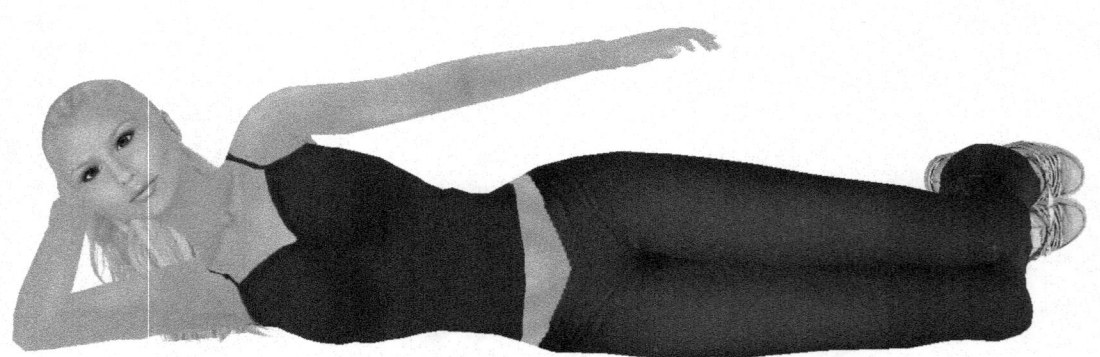

## Preparing Yourself Physically

**CH. 2**

Now bend to the side, lifting your shoulders off the floor and stretching your free hand towards your feet. Remember that you are bending at the waist to touch your foot, rather than just stretching out your arm. Control the movement and keep your chin off your chest. This exercise could also be performed standing up and bending side to side with or without weights in your hands.

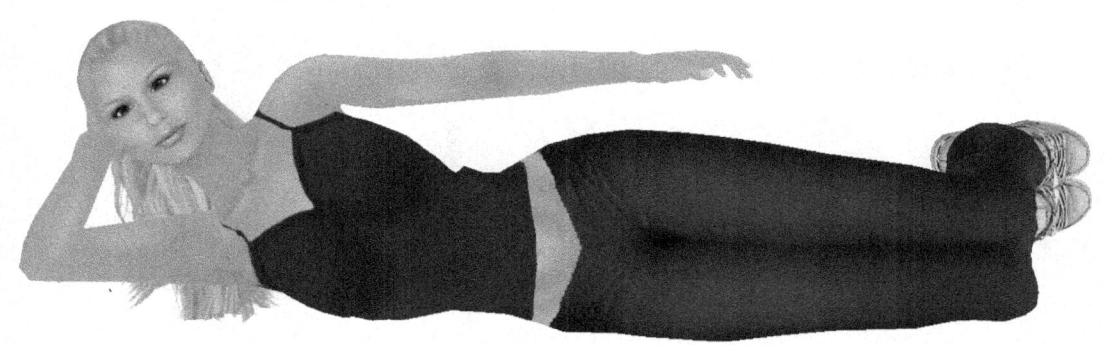

## The Lift

This exercise works both your abdominal and glut (or buttock) muscles. Lie on your back with your knees bent. Keep your hands by your sides throughout the exercise.

# Preparing Yourself Physically

Slowly lift your buttocks off the floor, keeping a straight line between your knees and lower back. You can vary the exercise by slowly lifting up your hips and then slowly setting them back down, or by leaving the hips up and slowly pulsing the hips upward. Do not lift up or down too quickly so you do not put unnecessary pressure on your lower back, and make certain to control the movement.

## The Squeeze

This one is tough! This exercise has four counts with a very distinct movement on each count.

1. Start with a regular abdominal crunch upwards.

2. Lift your hips up towards the ceiling.

## Preparing Yourself Physically

3. Squeeze everything together, pulling your elbows and knees together.

4. Release on 4 and repeat the sequence.

## Planks

This is a great exercise to work your abs, arms, back and legs. Start by lying face down on the floor with your hands by your shoulders palms down, and your toes against the floor as if you were about to do a pushup. Now use your abs to lift your hips, legs and upper body off the floor, resting your weight on your toes and your forearms. Try to make your entire body straight and flat like a plank of wood. Hold for thirty seconds.

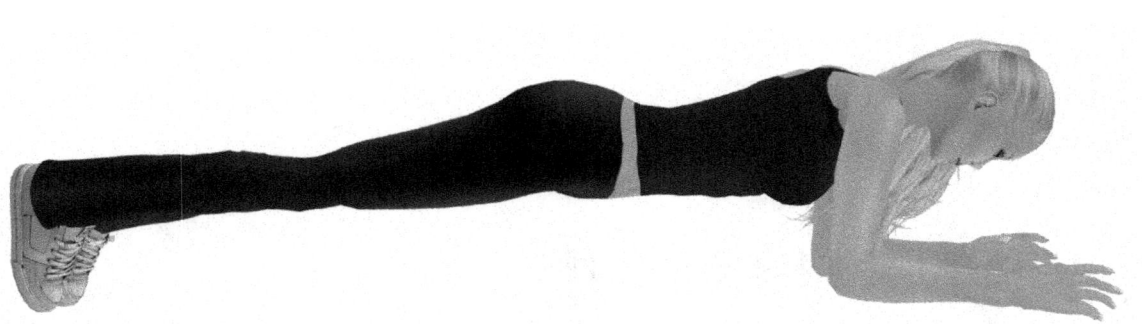

## Preparing Yourself Physically

Then roll sideways onto just one elbow to work your obliques (side abs). Hold for thirty seconds, then roll to the other elbow and repeat on the other side.

## ⭐ Becoming Flexible ⭐

1. Start with a light warm up for ten minutes (either jogging, briskly walking, riding a bicycle, several jumping jacks, etc.) This is very important, as it warms your muscles, making them more pliable and ready to be stretched.

2. While holding onto a chair or a wall, use your leg muscles to kick your right leg straight up in front of you. You should NOT be concerned with kicking high! The purpose is to further warm up your "kicking" muscles to make sure they are ready to be stretched. Do ten slow kicks on each leg, making sure to control the kick all the way up into the air as well as back down to the ground.

3. Now stand with your feet together and slowly bend over, trying to touch your palms to the ground while keeping your legs straight. Hold for one minute.

4. Straighten up, then cross one leg over the other at the ankles and bend back over, once again trying to touch your palms to the ground. Hold for thirty seconds, then switch legs and repeat.

## Preparing Yourself Physically

**Ch. 2**

5. Stand with your feet shoulder-width apart, then reach your right arm over your head (arm to ear). Bend your upper body sideways to the left. Hold for thirty seconds.

# CH. 2
## The Ultimate Guide to Dance Team Tryout Secrets

6. With feet still shoulder-width apart and your toes pointed forward, bend over to the left and try to touch your chest to your left thigh. You may want to hold onto your ankle or leg to hold you down in the stretch.

   Remember to keep your back straight, and hold for thirty seconds. Do not bounce, and only stretch to the point of tightness, not pain.

## Preparing Yourself Physically

**CH. 2**

7. In the same stretch, turn your left foot so that its toes point out to the side. Hold for thirty seconds.

Ch. 2 | The Ultimate Guide to Dance Team Tryout Secrets

8. In the same chest-to-thigh stretch, flex your left foot so that the toes are raised up in the air. You should feel the stretch move down into the calf (below the knee) of your leg. Hold for thirty seconds.

## Preparing Yourself Physically

**CH. 2**

9. Relax your left foot while still in the same stretch. Now rise up on the toes of your right foot. You should feel the stretch move into your hip/groin muscles. Hold for thirty seconds.

# CH. 2

## The Ultimate Guide to Dance Team Tryout Secrets

10. In the same chest-to-thigh stretch, keep your left leg straight and toes still pointed out to the side while carefully bending your right knee into a lunge. This focuses the stretch along the back of your left thigh, or hamstrings. Hold for thirty seconds.

## Preparing Yourself Physically

CH. 2

11. Now turn your left foot so that the toes once again point forward, then move your upper body to the center between both legs. Try to touch the floor between your feet with the palms of your hands. Hold for thirty seconds.

12. Straighten up, then repeat steps 5 through 11 on the right side.

13. Straighten up, turn your feet and knees out and sink into a deep plie or squat. Make sure your knees are over your ankles and not your toes to prevent injury to your knees. Put your hands on your thighs just above the knees, then use the weight of your upper body to push your knees open further. This helps stretch your inner thighs. Hold for thirty seconds.

## Preparing Yourself Physically

14. Holding the same center stretch, push your right shoulder forward while looking over your left shoulder. This stretches your back and right shoulder. Hold for thirty seconds, then repeat on the other side.

15. Now have a seat on the floor with your feet together and legs out straight in front of you. Flex your toes back towards you and try to hold them back with your hands if possible. You should feel the stretch in your calves, or the muscles that run along the back of your legs from below the knees to the ankles. Hold for thirty seconds.

# Preparing Yourself Physically    CH. 2

16. Sit up straight, then bounce your legs slightly to loosen them up. You should NOT be stretching in any way while doing this! This is simply to loosen up the muscles just stretched. Repeat stretch 15 once more.

17. Sit up straight and bounce your legs to loosen them up, then point your toes and repeat the stretch. Hold onto either your ankles or your legs to hold you down in the stretch for thirty seconds. Again, you should be trying to touch your chest to your thighs—touching your nose to your knees will only cause you to curve your back without stretching the muscles in your legs properly.

# CH. 2

## The Ultimate Guide to Dance Team Tryout Secrets

18. Sit up, bounce your legs slightly to relax the muscles, then repeat stretch 17 once more.

19. Sit up straight, then bring your feet in towards you with the bottom of your feet touching each other. Try to bring your feet in as close to you as possible while keeping your back straight. This is called the "butterfly" position because your legs look like wings on a butterfly. Use your hands to press your knees towards the ground and hold for thirty seconds.

## Preparing Yourself Physically

20. Now bend your upper body over your feet, focusing on touching your chest to your feet. Use your hands on your ankles to hold your feet in close to you, and press your elbows against your knees to hold your knees close to the ground at the same time. Hold for thirty seconds.

21. While still in stretch 20, use your thigh muscles to try to push your knees up against your elbows. At the same time, use your elbows to make sure that your knees don't actually rise up. Push hard with your thigh muscles and your elbows for 10-12 seconds, then relax. You should then be able to stretch even further over. Sit up straight and bounce your knees slightly to help relax the muscles just worked.

22. Straighten out your right leg. Point your toes, then bend over your right leg, working towards touching your chest to your thigh. Hold onto your right ankle to hold you down in the stretch for thirty seconds. Keep your back flat while performing this stretch. You should feel the stretch in your right hamstring, which is the muscle that runs along the back of your thigh.

# Preparing Yourself Physically

**CH. 2**

23. Sit up straight, flex your right toes back towards you, then repeat the stretch once more. You should feel the stretch move down into the calf muscle. Hold for thirty seconds.

24. Straighten your legs out to either side in what is called a "straddle". Your legs should be opened as far as is comfortable but not PAINFUL. Knees should be pointed up towards the ceiling, and toes should be pointed. Hold your arms out like a T, then lean your upper body from side to side in a see-sawing motion, stretching a little closer to each leg as you go. Do this several times to loosen up your back and hip muscles.

25. Now lean sideways over your right knee with your arm stretched over your head (your arm should be against your left ear). Try to touch your right ear to your right knee, and hold for thirty seconds.

26. In the same stretch, turn your upper body and try to touch your chest to your right thigh. Use both hands on your ankle to hold you down for thirty seconds. Make sure that you keep your toes on both feet pointed, and that both knees remain pointed towards the ceiling (don't let your left knee roll in towards the center). Also try to keep your back as flat as possible while in this stretch.

## Preparing Yourself Physically

**CH. 2**

27. Now stretch your upper body towards the center between your feet. Again, keep your back flat, toes pointed, and both knees pointed up instead of rolled in towards the center. It might take a while to achieve, but your ultimate goal here is to be able to lay your upper body flat on the ground.

28. Repeat stretches 22 through 26 over your left leg, holding each stretch for thirty seconds.

# CH. 2 — The Ultimate Guide to Dance Team Tryout Secrets

## Toe Touch Drill #1

This drill will help you build strong muscles for performing great center split leaps (also called Russian leaps) and other similar jumps.

1. Start by sitting in a straddle position on the floor with your hands braced on the floor in front of you.

## Preparing Yourself Physically

2. Lift your legs a few inches off the ground while keeping your torso straight, toes pointed, and knees pointing towards the ceiling. The quadriceps should be lifting, not your back muscles.

3. Hold for 5 seconds and then set the legs down.
4. Repeat the drill and work up to pulsing the legs 5 times a set.

## Toe Touch Drill #2

This is another drill to help strengthen your hip flexors (the muscles that lift your legs for toe touches and Russian leaps).

1. While seated in a straddle, brace your hands at either side of your left leg.
2. Lift your left leg two inches off the ground and circle your leg (as if drawing a circle in the air with your toes without bending your knee). Make 10 circles, then repeat on the right leg.
3. For an advanced version of this drill, brace your hands in the center and circle both legs at the same time.

## Preparing Yourself Physically

CH. 2

## Toe Touch Drill #3

This drill works both your hip flexors and your abs to increase your ability to do center split leaps (Russian leaps). Do not try to hold the straddle position; instead count out loud 1-2-3-4, hitting the straddle on 2 and lying on the floor for counts 1, 3 and 4.

1. Lie on your back on the floor with your arms straight up overhead and your legs stretched out flat, knees together.

2. In one movement, sit up while popping your legs out into a wide straddle and reach with both arms between your legs. Be careful not to bend your knees or overstretch!

3. Lie back down on the floor in the starting position.

## Preparing Yourself Physically

**CH. 2**

## Sitting High Kick Drill

This drill will help you build the muscles needed to perform great high kicks.

1. Sit on the ground with your right leg bent and your left leg out straight. With your left toes pointed, keep your left leg perfectly straight while you lift it hard towards your face (as if performing a high kick while sitting down). The kick should be performed quickly on the way up, and

slowly lowered back down to about two inches above the ground before being repeated. It is important that you do not bend your knee while performing this drill.

2. Do ten kicks, then rest your leg on the ground and lay your upper body over your bent leg to help further relax the worked muscles. Your ultimate goal is to work up to touching your nose or hitting your chest with your leg each time you kick.

## Preparing Yourself Physically

3. Sit up straight, then stretch your left leg out directly behind you. Use your hands and arms on either side of you to brace your weight in this position for thirty seconds. You should feel the stretch in your right thigh as well as in your left hip.

4. Push up into a deep left lunge, making sure your right knee is over your ankle, not your toes. Brace the weight of your upper body by placing both hands on the ground to the inside of your right foot. Try to push your left hip towards the floor without bending your left knee for thirty seconds. You should feel this stretch in your left hip flexor.

## Preparing Yourself Physically

5. Increase the stretch in your hip flexor by resting your left knee on the floor. Push your hips forward into the stretch, and hold your upper body straight up by bracing your hands on your right knee or thigh. Hold for thirty seconds.

6. Move the stretch down into your left quadricep (the big muscle that runs along the front of your thigh) by bending your left leg. Try to reach back with your left hand and grab your left foot if you can (if you can't, just bend your left leg as much as you can for now and work up to being able to eventually touch your left foot to your rear end). Hold for thirty seconds.

## Preparing Yourself Physically

7. Move the stretch into your right hamstring by releasing your left foot then sitting back on it. Straighten out your right leg and bend over it, trying to touch your chest to your right knee. Hold for thirty seconds.

# CH. 2
## The Ultimate Guide to Dance Team Tryout Secrets

8. Push your hips up and bend over to the left. Try to touch your chest to your left thigh. You may want to hold onto your ankle or leg to hold you down in the stretch. Remember to keep your back straight, and hold for thirty seconds.

9. Slide back down in a deep lunge; again making certain that your right knee is over your ankle and not your toes. This time try to place your elbows on the floor to the inside of your foot. Hold for thirty seconds.

10. Repeat this entire drill on the opposite leg.

## Front Splits

Stand up, then very slowly slide down into your right split. Keep your right foot pointed, and brace your weight with your hands on the floor to either side of your right leg. Remember to position your back leg as it will be required at the tryouts (either the knee should be turned under with the top of the foot on the floor, or the knee and foot may be required to be turned to the side so that the inside of the leg is on the floor). Only go to the point of tension, never pain. If at any point you begin to feel a

## CH. 2 — The Ultimate Guide to Dance Team Tryout Secrets

burning, pulling, or tearing sensation, get out of the splits immediately, as you may be overstretching and causing permanent damage, which could lead to permanent loss of flexibility. If your splits still have a ways to go before being flat on the ground, hold your splits for 1 to 1 and a half minutes. For splits that are all the way to the ground, hold them for five minutes to help maintain this flexibility.

If your splits are low enough to the ground, try to keep your back straight and as upright as possible. Not only does this present a prettier picture than someone who is hunched over their front leg, but it also shows your flexibility better to the judges. If your splits are all the way to the ground, sit with your arms out to your sides in a low V, fingers neatly together and the tips just barely touching the ground.

Keep in mind that for most people, it can take a great deal of time and work to achieve splits that are all the way to the ground. So be patient. Pushing your splits too far will only hurt your muscles and your flexibility, not help them! And don't forget to also perform your splits on your left leg as described above.

## Center Splits

To do your center splits, stand with your feet shoulder width apart, toes pointed out to either side. Now very slowly slide your feet out, making sure to brace your weight using your hands and arms in front of you. If your center splits are low enough but not all the way to the floor still, you may need to brace your weight on your elbows and forearms instead. Remember to only stretch to the point of tightness, not pain. Hold for 1 to 1 and a half minutes, or five minutes for center splits that are all the way to the ground. Once your center splits are flat on the ground, be sure to keep your toes pointed and knees turned up towards the ceiling, not rolled in towards the center. Also, be sure to sit up straight, shoulders back, chin slightly lifted.

# Ch. 2 — The Ultimate Guide to Dance Team Tryout Secrets

## Kicks

To have good kicks, not only do you need height in your kicks, but you also have to have good posture and technique. To start, stand with your back against a wall with a smooth surface that won't scratch your back. Place your hands on your hips with your fingers together. Keep your shoulders pulled back and down, and your chin slightly lifted.

Now start with waist high kicks, which consist of two parts: the prep and the kick.

**Prep:** With your feet together, bend your knees just a little.

## Preparing Yourself Physically

**Kick:** Use your stomach and leg muscles to kick your leg, straightening both knees as you do so. The toes of your kicking foot should be pointed during the entire kick.

Use the wall behind you to help you remember to keep your back straight as you prep and kick. A wall behind you will also help prevent you from swinging your kicking leg too far behind you before each kick.

As you get the hang of it, begin speeding up your kicks until there is no hesitation between each prep and kick. Practice kicking one leg properly for a bit, then switch to the other leg. Only kick to waist height right now, since it is more important at this point to master proper kicking technique before worrying about how high you can kick.

# CH. 2

## The Ultimate Guide to Dance Team Tryout Secrets

Once you have mastered kicking each leg properly, practice alternating your kicks back and forth between each leg without stopping in between the preps and kicks. Start off slowly with the following sequence: prep kick right, prep kick left, prep kick right, and so on. Gradually speed up until there is no hesitation between each step in the sequence. As you speed your kicks up, your prep will turn into more of a little hop, but be careful to control the prep. The prep should only be a small hop in place, not a big jump.

## Preparing Yourself Physically

**CH. 2**

Once you have mastered proper posture and kicking technique, you can then begin to work on properly performing kicks at various heights. Kicks start off at ground height, which is basically just pointing your toe in front of you with a straight leg, then graduate to waist height, up to chin height (the foot of each kicking leg should be level with your chin), and all the way up to full-out high kicks (good high kicks actually hit the brim of a hat if the dancer is wearing one!). Again, though, it is very important to remember to master each height level using proper technique before kicking higher. Work on mastering good waist high kicks first, then move up to chin high kicks, and so on. Don't worry if your high kicks aren't much higher than your chin high kicks right now... it takes a lot of strength and flexibility to achieve high kicks that "hit the hat" like the Kilgore College Rangerettes!

## Step Kicks

Once you have the basics of good technique with your back against a wall, it's time to learn how to do step kicks, which are often required at team tryouts.

For step kicks, as with regular kicks, you will usually be in a line with a small group of others. You will learn the details of how to "hook up" with the others to form a kick line at the tryout clinic. The important thing to remember when hooked up is to keep your fingers neatly together on each hand, and your thumbs tucked in close to your hand instead of like claws gripping the other person's shoulder. Your arms should also always be kept board straight—nothing looks sloppier to a judge than to see elbows that are bent!

## Preparing Yourself Physically

The sequence for performing step kicks is: step left, kick right, step right, step left, step right, kick left, and so on. Each step just before kicking should be flat footed, while the other two steps in between each kick should be up on the balls of your feet. As you step kick, it is helpful to keep the following words in your head: step kick, step, step, step kick, step, step, step kick... and so on.

When you are performing step kicks at the tryouts, usually you will be required to perform them with your side to the judges. This gives the judges a good profile view of your posture as you kick, allowing them to look for hunched backs and shoulders. Therefore, it is important that you work very hard to keep your back straight while performing step kicks. Also, be sure not to take overly large steps, as this will cause you to swing your kicking leg forward and up instead of just kicking it up, and points will be taken off your score.

As with regular kicks, practice doing waist high step kicks properly before moving up to the higher height levels. Remember the following key points: straight back, shoulders back and down (not hunched up towards your ears!), toes pointed on the kicking leg, lift each kick with your stomach and leg muscles, and never bend the knee of the leg being kicked. Other mistakes in poor technique to watch for are pushing your chin out when kicking, rolling up on the toes of your supporting/base leg during a kick, and bending the knee of your base leg too much while kicking the other leg.

## ☆Developing Dance Technique☆

Dance technique is certainly not developed overnight. There is a significant amount of time and dedication necessary to becoming a successful dancer. Luckily, there are many available sources that can assist you in becoming the very best dancer you can be. First of all, you should strongly consider enrolling in a dance class at a local studio if at all possible. For younger students, studios might combine jazz, ballet, and tap into an hour and a half class. For older students, most classes are available separately and are typically an hour long. If possible, you should try to take both a ballet and a jazz class. Why a ballet class, you might ask? Ballet is the basis for all types of dance and is the best stepping-stone to improving your technique. If the team director teaches at a local studio, you should certainly try to secure a place in his or her class. Also, as

## Preparing Yourself Physically

mentioned earlier, if the director teaches a dance class at the school you attend, you should try to work the class into your schedule so you can gain a sense of the types of dance that are emphasized by the director and become comfortable with the director's teaching style.

In addition to dance classes, you might want to look into some of the videos that are available on dance technique. Two good online catalogs to search for the latest and best dance technique videos are JustForKix.com and DiscountDanceSupply.com. Look specifically for videos on leaps, turns, dance conditioning, and beginner or intermediate level ballet technique, all of which will help you prepare for your tryouts.

Another good idea would be to check out a dance convention that may be in your area. Although these conventions can be costly, you are exposed to some of the best dancers and choreographers in the field of dance, and the learning experience is second to none. This is a great opportunity to learn exciting combinations, polish your technique, and also gain confidence when performing in front of and with strangers. As a dance team member, you are very much in the public eye and you need to be confident and secure in your ability as a dancer. The more opportunities

# CH. 2
## The Ultimate Guide to Dance Team Tryout Secrets

you give yourself to perform in front of an audience, the better you will be in front of the panel of judges. It will also help prepare you for the experience of having to learn a routine quickly while surrounded by other dancers, which you will also go through during your actual dance team tryouts.

Finally, as mentioned before, you absolutely should attend any workshop, clinic, or prep classes that the dance team may have. This will be your best opportunity to gain a sense of the types of dance that the team favors and also learn what you need to work on for the tryouts. In addition, you may be able to meet some of the dancers on the team that are willing to mentor you. The many advantages to attending one of these functions will greatly benefit you in the long run.

## ☆Probable Moves☆

There is little question that the level of dance ability that most teams require has certainly been raised over the years. It is very important that you have some of the basics down, as most teams will require you to execute the splits on both legs, high kicks, a single or a double pirouette,

## Preparing Yourself Physically

CH. 2

and a grand jeté/split leap. As I have judged dance team tryouts over the years, I have seen more and more teams requiring double turns, switch leaps, or axels in their tryout dances. Of course, this does not mean that all teams require these difficult elements, but this proves all the more reason to learn in advance what will be required to be a member of the team.

## Turns

It is almost a certainty that a turn, either a single or a double, will be in the tryout dance. The placement of your body is one of the most important elements in successfully completing a turn. To prepare, your shoulders and hips should be in alignment, shoulders pressed down, and there should be an even distribution of weight between both legs. When you begin to turn, do not "shrug" the shoulders up or crunch the torso. It is important to stay uplifted and tall and remember your arm placement. Your arms create force that helps you turn; however it is important to remember that you need to place the arms in towards the center of the body rather than throw them around. If your hips are out of alignment or you throw your arms, you will lose your balance and fall out of your turn.

Spotting is also crucial when you are learning how to turn. Luckily, there are many ways to practice spotting. To do this, find a place in the direction you are turning and keep your eyes focused on that one spot as you begin to turn. As you turn, whip your head around and find that spot again. Continue this exercise and stay focused on your spot to maintain your balance. Remain in relevé (up on the balls of your feet) throughout the turn and keep your body aligned and in control.

Finally, make certain that you remain on the ball of your foot for the entire turn. If you turn flat-footed, you will not be able to execute additional turns. The area behind your toes (called the "ball" of your foot), is your platform. If you spread your weight evenly among this area, you will have a better chance of maintaining your balance. However, before attempting more difficult turning elements, it is important that you

## Preparing Yourself Physically

perfect your single turn first. With an ample amount of practice on spotting and perfecting your body alignment, your single turn will eventually become a double or a triple turn.

## Leaps

In terms of leaps, many teams require a grand jeté (also called a split leap), and there a few basic rules to master before you move on to more complicated leaps. First of all, remember to control your body in the leap. Many beginning dancers feel that if they swing their arms wildly they will gain extra momentum. This is certainly not true. The strength to get height in the air for the leap comes from the plié. In addition to the plié being important for the lift to leap, you will also need to land in plié to avoid injury. If you jar your body by landing straight-legged, you run the risk of injuring your knees and lower back. Hip placement is also important...the hips need to face front rather than be lifted or turned in. Finally, lift your chin in jetés to gain additional height. Remember, if you look down, you go down.

## ☆Practice Makes Perfect☆

As noted before, the dance technique and fitness training will not happen overnight. You must commit to a program and rigorously train several months in advance of tryouts. Nothing comes easy, but you will feel much more confident if you follow these steps faithfully. There will be times that you will doubt yourself and what you are doing. That is only natural, and it happens to everyone. However, get past those days of frustration and remind yourself of your goal of making the dance team. You will feel much more confident going into tryouts after working hard on a training program, and you will have a distinct advantage over many of the other dancers. Just remember to be realistic and understand the time and dedication that are required to see real results. They will come in time. You just have to be patient and committed to your program.

# CHAPTER 3

# Preparing Yourself Mentally

**W**hen preparing for tryouts, the most beneficial element to have besides dance technique is confidence. Confidence in yourself, confidence in your ability, and confidence in making the team are the best assets on your side.

# CH. 3
## The Ultimate Guide to Dance Team Tryout Secrets

## ☆ Confidence ☆

If you go into a tryout thinking you are not going to make it, you are probably correct. It is not even enough to go into tryouts just thinking you can do it; you need to KNOW that you can. When you go in with your head held high, shoulders back, and a smile on your face, you are in a much better position to impress the judges.

It is completely understandable that not everyone is confident performing in front of people. Most judges do take into consideration that the dancers are nervous. However, if you get out there and show the judge

# Preparing Yourself Mentally

## CH. 3

that you are absolutely terrified by running out of the room in fear, the judges will certainly wonder if you are going to do that when a team performance comes around. Every person gets the "butterflies", but the people who can control it and take the auditions in stride are the people who will be out there dancing with the team after tryouts.

Some of the best advice I can offer for preparing yourself mentally is to have tunnel vision when you are at the pre-tryout dance clinic or at the actual tryout practice. In other words, do not spend all your time looking at the other dancers and comparing yourself to others. You end up not only losing your confidence, but you will also lose your focus on the routine that you need to learn. The only time you should check out the other dancers is when you are initially evaluating the team prior to tryouts at a team performance. When the tryout time rolls around, you will already know the level of dance that is to be expected, and you do not need to waste your time comparing yourself to everyone else. It is certainly possible that there might be someone who is a better dancer. However, what good is it to dwell on that fact? The only thing that you need to concentrate on is your own dancing and the tryout routine.

## Confidence Vs. Ego

There is also a huge difference between self-confidence and an overblown ego. Regardless if you are the best dancer there, you certainly do not want to offend the director or returning members who may have a say in your placement on the team. Be polite to other dancers and the instructors. A bad attitude sticks out like a sore thumb, and no one wants to be on a team with someone who openly complains about everything. Go into the tryouts with a positive attitude and let your personality shine. The judges will be able to see this when you audition, and judges love to see someone with the right attitude towards the team.

## ☆Focus☆

Focus is also an important element in preparing yourself. This can be accomplished by using the many resources out there, both in print and on the internet, that offer insight into the world of dance. This information will help you gain knowledge about dance technique, the dance industry, and will also offer additional advice on preparing yourself for tryouts. The dance industry is so much bigger than most people who are on the outside think. If you do an internet search on dance magazines or dance

## Preparing Yourself Mentally

company websites, the number of results returned will likely astound you. Take some time and go through these sites. Not only will you gain a great amount of knowledge, but it will also increase your focus during the dance team tryouts.

## ☆Motivation☆

Everyone uses different motivation techniques, but winners perceive events in ways that give them that special advantage toward success. The best way to accomplish this is to believe in yourself and your abilities. The more that you can visualize yourself being successful at tryouts and see yourself on the team, the better your mental state will be on the big day. In truth, you can practice only so much, but the extra edge you need just might come from the mental skills that you can develop.

A motivation technique that will help you in your dance team auditions as well as throughout life is to develop positive thoughts and dismiss those thoughts of fear and anxiety. The worst thing you can think is, "I can't do it," "I'm afraid," "I'll let everyone down if I don't make it," "I have not practiced enough". Those thoughts are self-defeating, create unnecessary stress, and will significantly get in the way of your success. Do not doubt your ability or think that everyone else trying out has a better chance to make the team. Be confident and give it your absolute best shot.

If you do begin to feel the stress creeping in, use it to your advantage. Nerves are natural and pressure is part of auditions, but they can ruin you if you let them take over. Instead of dwelling on how nervous you are, say to yourself that you are excited and ready for the challenge. Take charge of your feelings and let them motivate you to practice harder, focus more, and feel powerful. This will help you shift the stress to a feeling of being psyched up and determined.

Motivation can come from a variety of external sources as well. Some people write in journals, while others might be motivated from being in a group of people that have similar goals. Experiment with a variety of methods and find out which one works best for you. Here are few ideas that you might like to try:

## Preparing Yourself Mentally

**CH. 3**

★ Cut out articles or photos of dancers from dance magazines and post them around your room or keep them in your bag so you can see them often.

★ Make a poster collage of the team or other dance pictures to place on your wall.

★ Get with a group of friends to audition and practice together and keep each other motivated.

★ Visualize yourself on the team prior to bedtime. See yourself in the team uniform. This is also a great time to review the tryout routine in your head before you fall asleep.

★ Make a practice schedule along with weekly goals and stick to it. This will make you proud of what you have accomplished and motivate you to stay with the program.

The internal motivation techniques combined with the external sources will certainly give you a significant advantage. One final suggestion…if you do choose a group of friends that are also auditioning for the team as a motivation source, make absolutely certain that everyone can maintain a positive outlook toward the goal of making the team. Some people will inevitably let their nerves and negative thoughts get the best of them. Do not get caught up in this destructive pattern because negativity breeds negativity and you do not want any part of that! Therefore, if someone starts letting nerves or stress take over, let them in on the secrets that you have learned that help you maintain your focus.

# CHAPTER

## Preparing Your Appearance

hen you research the team, one of the first things you will need to learn about is the attire that the team requires for tryouts.

# CH. 4

## The Ultimate Guide to Dance Team Tryout Secrets

### ⭐ Audition Day Outfit ⭐

As mentioned before, this can range from a leotard with tights to t-shirts and shorts. It is important that you shop around and find a performance outfit that is both flattering and functional. While choosing the correct dance attire that is slimming and easy to dance in is not easy, it is an important process that will pay off in the end and impress the judges.

### Leotards

Not all dancers have the same body type, and a leotard that looks spectacular on one person may not look as good on someone else. This is why it is crucial that you do not pick a leotard just because it looks great in the catalog. You must try on several different styles to find what works best for you. Luckily, there are numerous styles of leotards to choose from, and you can find great dance clothes at several different places. Two popular online catalogs are DiscountDanceSupply.com and JustForKix.com. There are also many discount dance stores that offer dancewear for extremely reasonable prices.

## Preparing Your Appearance

If you are required to audition in a leotard, you will need to find one that will emphasize your positive aspects. The first element to consider is the type of fabric that you want. Lycra leotards that are shiny can draw more attention, but they also could make you look larger. On the other hand, a leotard that is made of cotton with a matte finish will make you look smaller. A cotton/lycra blend with a matte finish breathes well and is often very comfortable to wear when dancing.

In addition to fabric type, think about the color you want. There are many teams that require all black for auditions. However, if there is no specific color required, remember that dark colors are much more slimming than bright colors or pastels. If you decide to go with a colored leotard, do not select one that has more than 3 colors or your leotard will become distracting and take away from your performance. It is also a good idea to find a leotard that emphasizes the neckline and shoulders. However, if you have a large bust, avoid designs or bright colors that make the bust the focal point.

There are several different styles of leotards you can choose from. These styles include camisoles, tanks, halters, and short- or long-sleeved leotards.

It is important to remember a few basic rules of thumb when choosing your performance attire from these styles. Choose a leotard that creates an hourglass shape and uses diagonal designs rather than horizontal. A leotard that has a "V" waistline creates the illusion of a smaller waist and is very slimming. Keep in mind the "one-third, two-thirds rule" which states that a garment should cover either one-third or two-thirds of the body. This means that you should avoid a style that appears to divide the body in half. Long and lean is the best way to go, and the diagonal lines in V-necks and slanted hemlines at the hips are the most flattering in general.

## Fit

Fit is also extremely important in selecting a leotard. If your leotard is too small, it will look bad and be very uncomfortable. When you are restricted in your movement due to a leotard that is too tight, your performance will suffer significantly. I have always chosen a leotard that is a bit bigger for comfort, but of course you do not want your leotard to be baggy either. This is why it is so important that you try on a variety of sizes and styles to find the one that is just right for you.

## T-shirts and Shorts

If you are wearing a t-shirt and shorts for auditions, fit is also very important. You do not want your t-shirt to "swallow" you. Find a shirt that fits well and stays tucked into your shorts when you raise your arms. The shorts should also be a good length so you can move freely, yet remain properly covered. While in the dressing room, move around in your t-shirt and shorts, lifting your arms up and bending at the waist. Make certain that everything stays where it should so you will be comfortable and confident at the auditions.

## Jazz Pants

Jazz pants have undergone a radical transformation in the last few years, becoming very trendy and also very comfortable. The look these days are wide pants that flare at the bottom. The nice thing about this style of pants is that they are much more "forgiving" than the older style of jazz pants that taper down to the ankle, but you still need to find the pair that is right for you. Some pants are so wide and long that I have seen girls get caught up in them and trip during the tryout dance. Use caution when selecting this type of style. You certainly do not want to trip and ruin your performance because your pants were too long or too big! If you want to wear this style of pants for auditions, I would suggest a pair that has some room throughout the hips and thighs with a bootleg cut rather than wide-flare. You will still have the visual effect and the loose style works well for many figures, but a bootleg cut will be more practical for auditions.

While some dancers currently like to wear sweat pants that have been cut off below the knees Capri style, I strongly advise against wearing these at auditions. They may be comfortable and fun to wear during practices, but they do not have that polished look that will help you stand out in a positive way. They also tend to make you look shorter and accentuate the width of your hips and waist. Full length jazz pants are a much better choice for tryout attire.

## Underneath It All

Undergarments, including performance tights and a sports bra, are also important to your overall appearance. Shiny tights may be flashier, but they can also draw unnecessary attention to your legs and make them appear larger. A matte performance tight will be more attractive and draw less attention to your legs. Choose either black or suntan tights, and always have enough pairs handy in case you get a snag. If you are allowed

## Preparing Your Appearance

to audition in jazz pants, you will still need to wear the tights underneath. Finally, it is imperative that you wear a sports bra that has adequate support. This is especially true for those with larger busts.

## Shoes

The shoes that you choose to wear are just as important as your clothing. Some teams require dancers to audition in jazz shoes, while others allow tennis shoes. Either way, your shoes need to be broken in, and you must be comfortable performing in them. For jazz shoes, you may select the traditional type of jazz shoe or you can try a dance sneaker. The dance sneakers are like tennis shoes, but they have a split sole with a high arch. Some brands also have a "spin spot" to help your turns. These shoes are very popular with dance and drill teams. The most important thing to remember is to buy the shoes you will wear at auditions well in advance. You absolutely must have ample time to become comfortable dancing in them. Also, be sure to give them a good cleaning before the auditions.

## ⭐ Makeup ⭐

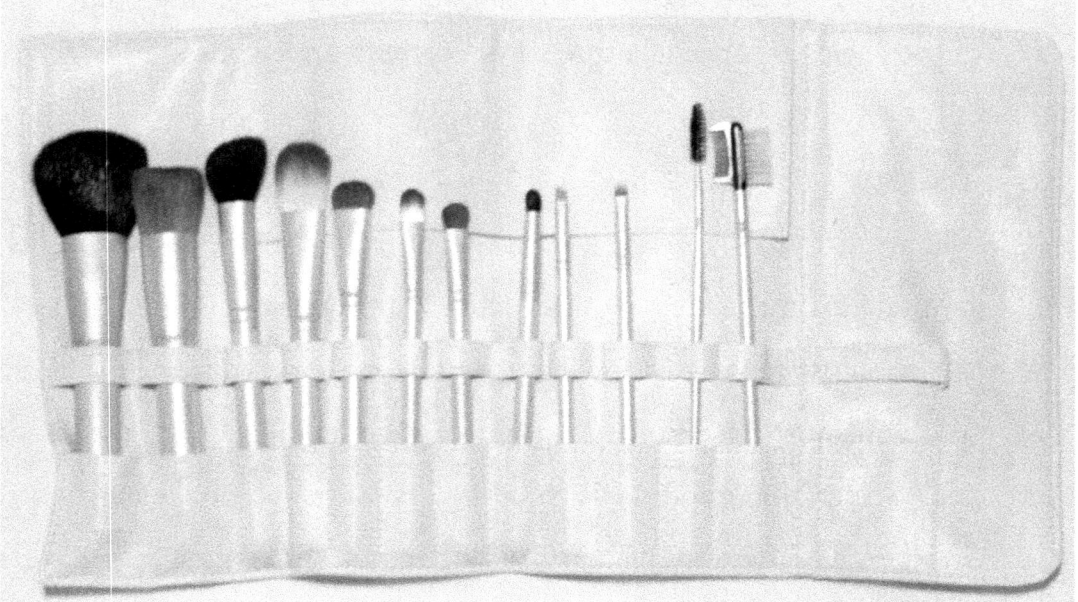

If you are not accustomed to wearing much makeup, it is a great idea to practice your makeup application ahead of time so you will know what to do for the auditions. It is important that your face stands out, but at the same time, you definitely do not want to look gaudy. Stage and performance makeup is very dramatic, but you can step it down a little for auditions because the judges are generally much closer to you than an audience would be.

## Preparing Your Appearance

**CH. 4**

When selecting your makeup, choose makeup that is waterproof and longwearing. There are many brands out there that offer these types of products, and they will make a big difference in your overall appearance. Makeup can look extremely tacky if it streaks the moment that you break a sweat.

## Foundation and Blush

For your foundation, choose a color that matches your skin tone, and blend well into your neck and jaw line. One tip that many makeup stylists use is to apply foundation to the eyelids as well. This not helps your eye makeup stay in place, but it also gives you a more uniform base color to apply eyeshadows to (which is especially helpful if you have visible veins above your eyes). You can introduce some color into your cheeks with blush. It is important to use blush in moderation, but you also do not want to look "washed out" by the lights. Apply either a pink or mauve blush to the apples of the cheeks, and blend toward the base of the nose.

## Eyes

You want your eyes to stand out, so the first rule is to use colors that keep the eye open. Begin by applying mascara, as this often flakes and smudges and can ruin your eyeshadow if you save it for last. Apply two coats of waterproof mascara, using an eyelash comb in between each coat to separate the lashes and remove clumps. Also, try applying your mascara to the bottom lashes first, and save the upper lashes for last. This will prevent your upper lashes from smudging mascara onto your eyelids when you look up to apply mascara to your lower lashes.

Further define your eyes by placing either a brown or taupe colored shadow in the crease of the eyelid. To open your eye, use a white or light colored shadow below your brow and on the inner half of the lid.

The next step is to use liquid or gel eyeliner, either black or brown, to line the upper eyelid. If the liquid eyeliner looks overly harsh, you could use a creamy pencil instead and smudge the line for a softer look. To line the lower lid, use a lighter application of either a shadow or pencil liner. Be sure not to connect the upper and lower lines at the outer corners...leaving these lines unconnected creates a more "open" appearance.

## Preparing Your Appearance

Also, don't forget to fill in and define your eyebrows. The softest and most natural way to do this is to simply use brown eyeshadow in a shade close to your hair color (or a few shades darker for blondes). Lightly brush on using short strokes that follow your natural eyebrow shape. If you go outside your eyebrow line, just use a napkin or sponge to gently wipe the extra shadow away.

## Lips

Finally, your lips are a big part of the look. The lips are important because you want the judges to see your smile even under bright lights and from several yards away. Start with a reddish brown lip liner that will both define and create the shape of your lips. You can make your lips look slightly larger by applying the liner just outside the lips, which is great for thin lips or balancing your lips (for instance, if you have a large lower lip and a thin upper lip, and vice versa). Fill in the lips with the lip liner to add staying power to your lip color. Then apply lipstick. A red shade will stand out and brighten up your look. When choosing a shade of red, try to find one that has a slight "blue" tint to it instead of a yellow or orange tint, as the blue tinted shades will make your teeth appear whiter. You will also want to try out various brands of lipstick ahead of time to find one that works well with your body's chemistry, as some shades may react when you wear them and turn orange after a few minutes on your lips.

Another quick tip is to smear a small amount of petroleum jelly across the front of your teeth just before your auditions. It may taste less than great, but it will ensure that even the driest of mouths will have no problem breaking into a smile during tryouts.

## Hair

Most teams require that you pull your hair away from your face for auditions. Use a simple rubber band, preferably one that matches your hair color, and jerk your head around a bit to ensure it will stay. There is nothing worse than having hair accessories fly around during auditions. Not only is it distracting, but it can also pose a safety hazard if someone were to slip on a ribbon or a rubber band.

## Warm-ups

Finally, do not forget that your appearance when you arrive for the auditions may be noted as well. To help keep your muscles warm while

## Preparing Your Appearance

you are waiting to audition, you will need to wear some type of warm-ups over your audition outfit. Do not wear sloppy clothes, and be sure to be organized as well. A good idea for presenting a great appearance is to have matching warm-ups and a dance bag to hold all your needed items for the big day.

Your appearance at tryouts is very important. It is certainly not a good idea to wait until the last minute to plan your audition wardrobe. Just as dancers have full dress rehearsals before any big performance, you should also practice in your tryout attire and full makeup a few times before the actual auditions. It would be terrible to learn at the auditions that you could not stretch or bend in your outfit, your shoes proved to be too tight or slippery to dance in well, or you found out that the type of eye makeup you chose drips into your eyes when you sweat! Get comfortable in your clothes and be confident in your shoes, as those are the last things you will want to worry about when the big day rolls around. Finally, more than anything else, your smile and your confidence are the best accessories you can have at auditions. Practice performing with both, and don't lose them when you step before the judges.

# CHAPTER 5

# Preparing the Paperwork

As discussed earlier, there will be several deadlines that you will need to adhere to for the dance team tryouts. Needless to say, it is rather important that you keep up with the dates and the required paperwork. The director certainly will want people on the team who can fulfill their responsibilities and complete work by the deadline, so you do not want to miss anything important. Directors do not like these two responses, "I did not know I was suppose to do that" and "No one

## Preparing the Paperwork

### CH. 5

told me". You do not want to start off on the wrong foot before you even audition for the team!

## ☆Dates and Deadlines☆

At the first meeting before tryouts, the director will typically hand out a paper with the tryout dates and the deadlines for the required forms. This paper is worth its weight in gold, and you do not want to lose it. You might even want to make an extra copy of the paper. Also, it is wise to immediately transfer the important dates to a calendar or a datebook that you review often. Plan your time accordingly so that you will not become overwhelmed and have to rush to compile any required forms.

Some of the dates you will have to remember include the parent/guardian pre-tryout meeting, any pre-tryout clinic dates, and also when the actual tryout practice will begin. There may be an audition run-through before the big day so everyone will be comfortable with the tryout process. Some teams even have a mock tryout a few days before the actual auditions for friends and family to view. If this is the case, be sure to let everyone know the date so they can come and cheer for you!

# ☆Time Management☆

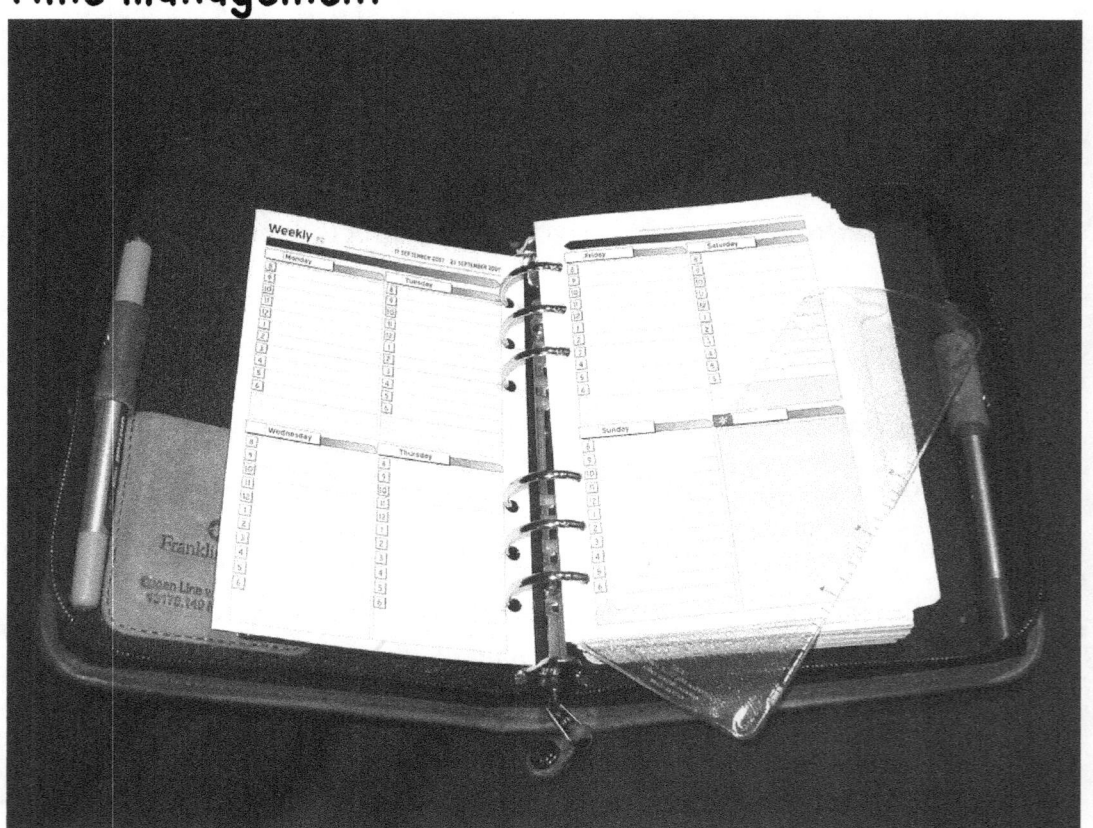

If you are juggling tryouts with schoolwork, time management is certainly important, and you will definitely need a plan. A great way to plan is to put all the important dates of schoolwork and tryout deadlines on a calendar. It is preferable to use a monthly calendar rather than a weekly calendar so you can see everything that is coming up for the month. The

## Preparing the Paperwork

next step is to work backwards and plan how much time you will need for each activity. Make a notation such as "Start studying for test" or "Practice high kicks" on the days that you designate, and do your best to stay on schedule so you can successfully complete everything.

## ⭐ Working with Teachers ⭐

If part of the tryout requirements include a grade check and teacher recommendation forms, do not put this off to the very end. Teachers are busy people, and if you present a form to them at the last minute that they must fill out and submit, they will not be especially happy with you. Allow them enough time to make an honest assessment of you and your ability to be involved in extracurricular activities. It is a good idea to start a list of the teachers who have or have not returned the recommendation form to the director. A teacher may honestly forget to turn in the form with all the other work they have to do, but a friendly reminder will be welcome if necessary.

As minor as the paperwork and deadlines may seem at first, they are in fact very important and can cause an enormous amount of unnecessary

## Ch. 5 — The Ultimate Guide to Dance Team Tryout Secrets

stress if you do not keep up with everything. You already have a tryout dance, correct attire, smiling, high kicks, etc. to worry about during this time. Do not add any other elements into the mix by forgetting deadlines or not turning in the required forms. Just get a system together early that you can work with, make sure that you stick with it, and be responsible. Not only will you impress the director, but you will also free up your time to work on the other important things that will land you a place on the team!

# CHAPTER 6

## Tryout Practice Day Tips

You have researched the team and you have completed all the necessary paperwork. So now what? If you have decided that you are ready and willing to dedicate the time to the team and would like to be a member, the next step is to attend the tryout practice.

# CH. 6

## The Ultimate Guide to Dance Team Tryout Secrets

### ⭐ Length of Time ⭐

The tryout practice can range from two days to one week. If the tryout practice lasts only a day or two, you will need to be able to learn the dances quickly. However, the dance you will have to learn will likely not be too long. On the other hand, if the tryout practice is longer, such as a week, you will likely have to learn more than one routine.

Regardless of the amount of time you will have to learn and perfect the tryout dance, you will need to be able to pick up the choreography and successfully follow along in practice. Staying focused on your dancing, the tryout routine, and your goal of becoming a member of the dance team will get you through the audition process. Therefore, let us start at the very beginning of tryout practice so that you will understand how best to focus on your ultimate goal of making the team.

### ⭐ Preparation ⭐

The first rule about dance teams is to be on time and prepared for practice. Do not show up dressed in jeans at the exact time that practice begins and ask if you can go and change. That is certainly not the way to start off with the director or the returning members. If the director has any say about your place on the team, I can guarantee you that your punctuality to practice will be included in the decision. If you are on time and ready to go, you are telling the director that you are taking the tryouts seriously, and you will impress them with your preparedness. I would highly suggest arriving at least 15 to 20 minutes early so that you can register, stretch, change clothes if needed, and get focused.

## ☆Getting Down to Business☆

It is important to remember that teams are operated like a business and not a social club. There is certainly time for fun, but that happens after the job for the day has been completed. Time is a scarce resource for dance teams, and every minute of the rehearsal is necessary. This also goes for the tryout practice, and it is time to get down to business the second you step in the door. Therefore, this is definitely not the time to catch up with your friends. You will have plenty of time after practice to chat, but tryout practice is just not the place. If your friend cannot resist speaking to you during tryouts, nicely tell him or her that you really need to concentrate on the routine and would love to talk after practice. Another idea is to explain this to your friends before practice begins and then learn the tryout dance on the other side of the room by yourself.

## ⭐ Attitude ⭐

If you do discuss the tryouts with your friends after practice, please do not openly complain or talk about the other people who are trying out. I can assure you that this will get back to someone, and you do not want to be viewed as a person who does not have a good attitude or is not a team player. There are some teams that allow returning or exiting members to have a say in who makes the team, and they will not look kindly upon you if you are already complaining before the audition. The best thing to do is to walk in the door to practice with a positive attitude and maintain that attitude throughout the entire process. Be nice to everyone and show respect to the officers, the director, and any returning or exiting members. Your kindness and respect will be appreciated and will get you further than a sour attitude at practice.

## Tryout Practice Day Tips — CH. 6

### ⭐ Positions Please ⭐

When practice begins, it is okay if you do not want to stand in the very front. However, try not to stand too far in the back where you may be blocked from viewing or cannot hear the instructor. This is not the time to be shy, and you are the only one who can make certain that you learn the dance. If you have a question or do not understand a move exactly, do not feel uncomfortable about raising your hand and asking the instructor to clarify. However, try not to ask about every single detail until the instructor has gone over the move again, and do not irritate the instructor by asking a question that has already been asked.

## ☆Focus☆

Please remember that this is your time to learn the dance and not the time to check out the other dancers. As mentioned in the Motivational section, there is very little to gain if you are looking around and comparing yourself to everyone else. If you do this during the instruction time, you will miss something the instructor has shown or explained. Needless to say, that would be truly detrimental to your success in making the team. Not only will you miss something important, but you will also compromise your confidence on something that you can do nothing about. Just focus on being the best dancer YOU can be, because the judges will evaluate each and every person who is auditioning for the team equally.

## ⭐ Memorization Tips ⭐

A good idea to help you remember the choreography is to have someone videotape the instructor performing the routine. You will need to ask if this is allowed. If it is, have a friend come at the end of practice and videotape the dance. This will be a great help to you because you will be able to carefully watch how the instructor performs the routine, and of course you will be able to review the dance for memory. In addition to the video, it is VERY important to bring a blank music CD to practice so that you can record the audition song. This is almost always allowed, and a CD of the music will allow you to practice the dance at home. In addition to actually standing up and practicing the dance, it is also helpful to have the music to visualize the routine. Take some time (perhaps prior to bedtime) to listen to the music and visualize the moves. It is worth it to take a few minutes and review the dance every night, because once you can actually see yourself performing the dance with no memory mistakes, you are able to polish the moves and perfect your showmanship.

In addition to practicing, try actually writing out the dance on paper. This can take some time, but you will find that the time is well spent. Not only will this help you learn the dance better, but you will also have a copy of the dance handy just in case you forget something while you are practicing. There are several methods of writing out dances, and everyone has a different style. You can write out the dance by every 8 count, use tick marks, draw stick figures to help you remember various poses on certain beats, or you can use any other system you create. Also, feel free to use certain words or phrases that help you to remember the dance better. The main goal of writing out the dance is to find a good system that is beneficial to you.

## ☆Turn It ON! ☆

In dance team practice, you are likely to hear the phrase "practice how you will perform it". This certainly rings true! It is never too early to begin practicing how you will actually perform in front of the judges. You will also hear at times, "just mark it for memory". This is acceptable as you are going through the dance with counts, but you absolutely need to turn it on when the music starts. Do not let yourself get comfortable performing the routine at a 50% level. You would be surprised how many people do this. They get so used to performing the routine at 50% that they actually perform that way at tryouts or at a performance. Always perform the dance with enthusiasm, a big smile, and as much energy as possible. The more you perform "full out", the better you will do before the judges.

## ⭐It's All in the Details⭐

When you are practicing the dance outside of the formal tryout practice, try to have someone videotape you performing the routine. There are some things that may surprise you, and you may not be aware of something that you are doing incorrectly. This is the time to think about the important elements of technique that make a big difference in your overall performance. For example, are you pointing your toes? How is your posture during a high kick? Are your legs straight in your jeté? Are your arms in control? Watching yourself perform will allow you to see exactly what you need to work on before the big day. Study your movements and take the time to make corrections.

If it is difficult to get a videotape of your performance, you could always ask someone to watch you perform the dance and give you an honest critique. Consider asking a returning member if they could offer some pointers on how to perform the dance better or if there are any other technique elements that you may need to improve. A returning member will likely be flattered that you are asking for help, and they just might be able to set aside some extra time before or after practice to work with you. Returning members are a great source of information, and they can definitely offer tips to help you best prepare for auditions.

## ⭐What to Wear⭐

Some teams will require certain attire for tryout practice. This is something that you will need to know early on so you can be prepared. If they do not require anything specific, take the time to make sure that you can move freely in your chosen outfit. Do not wear anything to practice that is uncomfortable or difficult to dance in, because you do not want to

## Tryout Practice Day Tips

worry about your clothing while you are learning the dance. Take special care to look nice at practice just in case the director is watching. Carry yourself well with your shoulders back and head held high. If you look terrified and embarrassed in practice, your readiness to perform with the team may be questioned.

You will also need to wear the shoes that you intend to audition in so you can practice the dance and feel comfortable in your shoes. When auditioning for my officer position my senior year, we had a "mock tryout" in the gym that we were going to use for auditions. To my horror, the floor was very different from the one we had used for practice, and I was sliding everywhere in my jazz shoes. Needless to say, I had to make a last minute adjustment, and I was so thankful that I had an opportunity to discover the problem before the tryouts. If you are practicing on a floor that is different from the one you are actually auditioning on, ask the director if you can have a chance to check out the other floor. He or she will likely not have a problem with this and will understand your concern.

## ⭐Breathe! ⭐

Finally, stay calm and focused. As mentioned before, your focus and confidence is such a huge part of the process. If you can keep your "eye on the prize", you will be ready to tryout. Make sure that you know the dance backward and forward, and take the time to work on the technique elements that will give you the extra edge you need for the judges. The worst thing that can happen is for you to succumb to the pressure and stress. Remember your positive attitude and remember why you decided to try out for the team in the first place. If you can do that, you will succeed during the tryout practice and be prepared for the audition day.

# CHAPTER

## Audition Day Tips

The big day has finally arrived! Today is the day that you finally have the opportunity to put all of the hard work and preparation to the test. The first thing you need to do is to relax. I know that this is very easy to say and a bit more difficult to actually do, but do not hinder your performance by becoming overly worked up and stressed out. Be confident in the fact that you have done all that is possible to prepare and you are ready for the audition. After all the hard work that you have done, you certainly do not want feelings of self-doubt to undermine your confidence.

## ⭐ The Night Before Tryouts ⭐

The night before, try to get a full eight hours of sleep. Although you may be anxious and excited, you will feel so much better if you are well rested for the auditions. Also, do not eat anything heavy the night before. Eat healthy and eat early, as it is sometimes difficult to sleep if you eat too late at night. After working so hard and making it this far, you certainly do not want to go before the judges feeling sluggish as a result of a stomach full of pizza.

Take a few minutes before bedtime to review the dance with the music. You could either visualize the dance or actually get up and mark the routine. Once you are confident with your memory of the dance, think about how you will actually perform. It is helpful to visualize yourself before the judges with a big smile and all the confidence in the world. Remind yourself that it is your time to shine and you have worked hard to get where you are. Use some of the motivational techniques discussed

## Audition Day Tips

earlier so you can wake up the day of the audition and know you are able to give it your best shot.

## Triple Check It

I would also highly recommend that you take the time to double and triple check that you have everything you need to take to the audition. The worst thing that could happen to your focus would be to run around the day of the tryouts trying to find your dance clothes or shoes. If you already have everything packed and ready to go the night before, the only thing you will have to think about is the dance you will be performing to perfection. In addition, it is a very good idea to remove your jewelry and leave it at home. Jewelry is often not allowed during tryouts, and you do not want to risk losing anything valuable by leaving it in the dressing room.

There are several items you want to bring to the auditions. First of all, remember the saying "if it can happen, it will happen". Therefore, you should certainly plan that you will get a great big hole in your tights as soon as you put them on! Never fear, just calmly go and get the extra pair that you remembered to pack. Some dancers will even bring two extra pairs to auditions just to be on the very safe side. In addition to an extra pair of tights, remember to pack every part of your tryout uniform, including your leotard or t-shirt and shorts, and of course do not forget your dance shoes.

## Beauty Items

In terms of beauty items, set aside the makeup that you will wear and the items you will need for your hair. You will definitely need to bring plenty of bobby pins and other hair fasteners, such as clips and rubber bands. In addition, bring plenty of hair spray because you do not want your hair to fall out of place. You might even want to bring along some hair or body glitter, if this is allowed at your tryouts. These items have become extremely popular, and teams are getting glitzier every year. If you do decide to go with face or body glitter, please make absolutely certain that the glitter is for the body or face and not just regular glitter. Some products are NOT for the eye area and can be very dangerous. Therefore, please read the labels and any warnings on the product before you buy anything. Biogime sells some fantastic products especially made for dance and drill teams, so you might want to look into their products to give yourself some extra glamour for the auditions.

Audition Day Tips

## Dancer Fuel

In addition to your clothes, makeup, and hair items, bring along some snacks that will help you keep your energy up. The audition process is typically long, especially if there are callbacks, and you do not want to become weak from hunger. Some snacks that are easy to take along could include fruit, power or granola bars, or even raw vegetables like carrot or celery sticks. You will also need to pack a few bottles of water to drink so you will be alert and hydrated. Do not snack on chips, cookies, or sodas because those foods can weigh you down and possibly make you sick to your stomach. Think healthy!

## ☆Tryout Day☆

When you do arrive at the auditions, go in with the confidence that you have built up and do not lose it when you get around everyone else. There will be some people who will not be as well adjusted to the pressure as you are, and you do not want to let their own self-doubt and fear affect you in any way. The best way to handle this situation is to nicely tell them that you need to prepare for the audition on your own and that you cannot wait to discuss everything after the tryouts. Then just take out your music player and listen to some music as you put on your makeup and fix your hair. An MP3 or portable CD player is great to bring along not only for some

## Audition Day Tips

peaceful reflection time as you are getting ready, but you can also listen to the audition music a few more times to practice or at least visualize yourself performing the routine. Everyone has their own way of preparing before an audition, but the most important thing to remember is to not get bogged down by other people's nerves and anxiety. We have discussed the importance of focus several times, and this is the time that you need it the most.

It is very important that you keep your muscles warm and limber when you are waiting to go before the judges. Simple jumping jacks or even running in place to warm up is perfectly acceptable. It is important that you warm up briefly prior to stretching so you do not injure yourself. When you do begin your stretches, use this time to relax and concentrate on getting your body ready to dance. Focus on your breathing and hold your stretches so you will get the maximum impact of the stretch.

The time has finally arrived! Your number has been called and you are lined up with your group to go in front of the judges. When you walk out with your group, make certain that you give the judges the best possible first impression. Walk out with your head held high, your shoulders back,

# CH. 7 — The Ultimate Guide to Dance Team Tryout Secrets

and a big smile on your face. Be confident and know that you are ready. The typical procedure for tryouts is to come out in a straight line with your group and face the judges for a few moments. This allows the judges to take note of your number and get a quick look at you. You will then be told to stagger your lines and take your beginning position. When the music comes on, perform with your best showmanship and technique, making certain to smile and make eye contact with the judges. Do not look down or count out loud, as this makes you seem nervous and unsure of yourself.

If you happen to make a mistake, do not panic! The absolute worst thing you could do if you falter on a step is to show it on your face and stop dancing. To be completely honest, judges might not even catch your mistake if you keep smiling and jump back into the dance immediately. Unfortunately, some people will become so consumed with thinking about the error they made that they cannot even finish the dance. A judge is not going to immediately cut you from the team if you make a simple mistake and they see it, but it very much depends on how you handle it.

## Audition Day Tips

**CH. 7**

When I judge a tryout, I always find it difficult to understand when someone makes a mistake and covers their face while running out of the room. Not only does that tell a judge a great deal about that person's ability to handle stress, but it is also very rude to the others in the group. Needless to say, the other dancers will find it a bit difficult to focus on their performance if someone is bolting out the door! The best way to handle a mistake is with maturity and grace. If you can demonstrate these attributes, the judges will be impressed that you were able to finish the routine without the mistake affecting the rest of your performance.

When you finish the dance, hold your pose for a few moments until you are told to recover. Stand up straight with your hands either pressed flat against the side of your thighs or else behind your back (depending on what instructions you were given by the director beforehand), and smile at the judges. This is the time that the judges write their final comments and determine the points to mark on your score sheet. To give you an idea of what the judges might be looking for, let us take a look at an example of a generic score sheet.

# CH. 7

**The Ultimate Guide to Dance Team Tryout Secrets**

## ☆ Sample Judges' Score Sheet ☆

| Category | Points |
|---|---|
| **Jazz Dance (40 points)**<br>　-Technique<br>　-Dance ability<br>　-Execution<br>Comments: | \_\_\_\_\_ |
| **Kick Routine (30 points)**<br>　-Technique<br>　-Flexibility<br>　-Control<br>Comments: | \_\_\_\_\_ |
| **Showmanship (15 points)**<br>　-Memory<br>　-Smile and Projection<br>　-Confidence<br>Comments: | \_\_\_\_\_ |
| **Grades, Teacher/Director Recommendation (15 points)** | \_\_\_\_\_ |
| Judge's Signature<br><br>_____ | Total<br><br>\_\_\_\_\_ |

## Audition Day Tips

As you can see from this example, there are two routines that are being judged, and the jazz category is worth slightly more than the kick routine. There are several elements that the judges will be looking at, and they can also make comments on the score sheet. More often than not, showmanship has its own category, and in this case it is worth 15 points toward the total score. This is such an easy category to master, and if you work on the motivation and confidence techniques, there is no reason not to get the full amount of points. In addition, this team gives points for grades and teacher recommendations. Of course, every team has their own system in determining how grades will be involved, but many teams do factor in grades and teacher forms as part of the final score. Remember that all teams use different types of scoring, and this is merely an example based on several of the score sheets I have seen over the years. The director might give you a sample score sheet prior to auditions. However, if it is not provided, the director will likely not mind if you ask how the scores are broken down on the score sheet.

# CH. 7 — The Ultimate Guide to Dance Team Tryout Secrets

## ☆ Callbacks ☆

After you have completed your audition, you will return to the dressing room and wait for the other groups to finish. After all the groups have performed before the judges, there may be callbacks. Please understand that if you get called back, it is not a definite yes or no for your status on the team. There could be many reasons why you were called back. First of all, a judge might not have been able to get a satisfactory look at you to give you the correct amount of points. A judge might also want to see someone who made a mistake to see how his or her memory fares the second time around. You will not know the exact reason for the callback, so there is no reason to speculate. I suggest you view this as just one more opportunity to show off. Walk out there before the judges with the same confidence as before and SHINE!

Once the auditions are over and you are waiting for the results, do not dwell on your performance. Know that you did your absolute best, and be patient while the administrators complete the tabulation of the score sheets. Waiting for the results is certainly the most difficult part of the entire process. Rather than panicking on what you might have made a

## Audition Day Tips

mistake on, take the time to reflect on what you actually did accomplish. Be positive and take heart in knowing that the many months you spent preparing for the audition were well worth your time and effort.

# CHAPTER 8

# After the New Team Announcements

**T**he moment is finally here and the new team announcements have just been posted. Regardless of the results, it is very important that you keep your dignity and accept the decision gracefully.

## After the New Team Announcements

**CH. 8**

Teams have a variety of ways to announce the new members. They may call out the names or audition numbers for the dancers who were chosen for the team, post a list of the new team members' names on a door, or they might give the new members an item such as a rose or a stuffed animal that represents their team. They may also pass out envelopes with letters inside stating whether you made the team.

# Ch. 8

## The Ultimate Guide to Dance Team Tryout Secrets

If you are fortunate enough to make the team, congratulations! You are about to embark on a very exciting time, and your hard work paid off in the end. While it is certainly expected for you to be very happy and excited about your accomplishment, it is important to remember the other dancers who did not make the team. Be kind to the dancers who were not selected, and save the exuberant celebration for a little later when you are alone with the other new team members.

There will typically be a new team meeting either immediately following the announcements or shortly thereafter. At this meeting, there are introductions and the director will give you information on uniforms, payments due, etc. There is almost always a ceremony of some type following tryouts to induct the new members to the team. Some teams keep secret what the ceremony entails, while others will hold a tea or slumber party for the new members. At my school in Waxahachie, the returning members would "kidnap" the new members out of bed in the morning and take them to practice at the football field. Of course the new members had to go in their pajamas with messy hair and no makeup. After practice the new team would head to a local restaurant and have breakfast. It was always a great time, and while some new members were

# Ch. 8 — After the New Team Announcements

aware of the induction, they never knew exactly when it would happen, so it was always a surprise.

If you were not selected to be a member of the team, be confident in knowing that you gave it your best shot and absolutely do not give up. There are many dancers who do not make a team right away, but if you keep your head up and accept the decision with dignity, you will be a stronger person. It is important that you do not tie your self-worth in with the decision of the judges, because you are not any less of a person if you do not make the team. Do not feel that everyone will be disappointed with you or that you let someone down.

Also, do not be rude or hateful to the dancers who were selected. This is certainly not the way to go. Do not accuse anyone of playing politics or talk about someone on the team behind their back. If you take the high road, you will be highly regarded for your maturity and grace.

Another option if you are not selected as a team member is to ask the director about becoming a team manager. Not only will you have the chance to be involved with the team, but you will also learn a great deal about the organization that may come in handy when the next audition comes along. As a manager, you will be able to see how the team trains and perfects their technique. This might give you some ideas that will help you prepare and improve your own technique for next time.

Take the time to reflect on the knowledge that you have gained from this experience and turn your frustration into determination for the next audition. It is almost certain that you learned quite a bit about dance and how the entire tryout process works. You will have a significant advantage next time when you audition, and that should give you some comfort. Just remember, Michael Jordan did not make his high school basketball team the first time. He turned that frustration around and with some hard work and serious determination, just look at what he has accomplished!

# ABOUT THE AUTHOR

Summer Adoue-Johansen's involvement in dance has spanned over 20 years and includes training in jazz, ballet, tap, and hip hop.

Before beginning her career in dance and drill team, Mrs. Adoue-Johansen was involved in cheerleading from 1990-1992 in her hometown of Waxahachie, Texas, and was selected as a UCA All-Star Cheerleader. After the experience gained from cheerleading, she turned to drill team and became a member of the Waxahachie H.S. Cherokee Charmers from 1992-1994, for which she also served as a

Senior Lieutenant. During her time as a Cherokee Charmer, Mrs. Adoue-Johansen received numerous awards including All-American, Dance Company, Kick Company, Outstanding Girl, and was also a finalist for Miss American High Kick.

Mrs. Adoue-Johansen continued her passion for dance and drill team as a member of the Texas Aggie Dance Team at Texas A&M University in 1996, where she also completed her degree in political science with a minor in business administration. In 1994, Mrs. Adoue-Johansen joined the staff of American Dance/Drill Team School and has taught and choreographed for numerous high schools and junior teams throughout the country. She currently serves as a camp manager and a head instructor for American Dance/Drill Team School® summer camps and has enjoyed guiding dance teams to reach their full potential.

Since 1996, Mrs. Adoue-Johansen has served as an adjudicator at dance competitions on both the state and national level. She has judged countless dance team auditions for high school and junior teams and has helped many dancers prepare for auditions.

## About the Author

Mrs. Adoue-Johansen is also a certified fitness instructor through The Cooper Institute in Dallas, Texas, and enjoys dancing to keep healthy and stay in shape. In addition to her love for dance, Mrs. Adoue-Johansen enjoys creating company websites and manages the extensive site for American Dance/Drill Team School®. She currently lives in Houston with her husband Espen and continues to train at local dance studios to update her technique and skills. She truly believes in the benefits of team sports and credits much of her own success to her involvement with dance teams. She is also Head Coach for a cheerleading program in Houston, Texas, which won back-to-back National Championships with American Cheer Power Texas State Championship three years in a row, where they also received the prestigious high-point award for the highest ranking cheer program. Her team has also been highlighted in numerous articles in several Houston publications for their quick rise to excellence and perfection.

www.ingramcontent.com/pod-product-compliance
Lightning Source LLC
Chambersburg PA
CBHW081355040426
42451CB00017B/3456